You Are

NOT

Alone

Living With

Dementia

Martha Geisler Patterson, Esq., CELA*

Certified Specialist in Trusts, Probate and Estates

***Certified as an Elder Law Attorney by the National Elder Law Foundation**

Published by Geisler Patterson Law
Anaheim, CA
www.ElderLawMom.com

TABLE OF CONTENTS

About Martha Geisler Patterson

I am Southern California's only TRIPLE Certified Caregiving Counselor.

Personally, I cared for my husband who died from Alzheimer's and Vascular Dementia, was part of the family team that cared for his mother who also died from Dementia, and the only child who cared for my mom who was widowed when I was 16.

I have helped over 1000 families … stay out of court and get the best care for their loved ones.

I am California State Bar Certified in Trusts, Probate and Estates, this means I have been certified as an expert at helping families with their Wills, Living Trusts, Powers of Attorney for Finances and Health Care, Probates, and Conservatorships.

I am Nationally Certified as an Elder Law Attorney which means I am an expert in Medi-Cal Planning, Medicare, Veteran's Benefits, Special Needs Trusts, basically everything related to caring for someone who lives with Dementia or Disability. I am a Certified Dementia Practitioner and Trainer.

I decided to go to law school and wanted to be a litigator. After earning my law degree, I spent the first ten years of my practice as a Deputy City as a successful litigator, winning all my cases.

Once I married and had a young family, I left litigation and really started learning Estate Planning and Elder Law.

I am forever grateful that I was able to learn from my mother in-law's failed trust, how to fix my mom's trust, and that I was able to plan for myself so that when my husband faced dementia (which caused his death at 66) I was prepared.

Chapter 1: Is it Alzheimer's or Dementia?

Understanding Alzheimer's and Dementia

Alzheimer's is one form of Dementia. Dementia is the "big umbrella" and there are many forms of Dementia. Alzheimer's is the most common form. Other common forms are Vascular Dementia (caused by a stroke or multiple trans ischemic attacks "mini strokes"), Frontal Temporal Dementia, Lewy Body Dementia, Parkinson's Dementia,

Is it Dementia or My Imagination?

The picture on the front cover is my mother in-law, husband, and brother in-law, and me. I was a caregiver, the attorney and daughter in-law of Doris who had Alzheimer's. This kit includes lessons I learned from her mother in-law, and from my mother who remained sharp until the last year of her life when some very small strokes took a bit of her memory and ability to understand away.

I have learned some ways to identify dementia and to help others. This kit provides information I have acquired from observing and helping many families so these are signs from the perspective of an Elder Law Attorney who has had to help not only herself, but hundreds of families face the awful truth that a loved one has dementia or Alzheimer's.

1. Repeating the same story
I know we all do this to some extent. We have our favorite tales of our childhood, our children, of days gone by, so we tell the story over and over. The repetition that goes with dementia is subtly different. It is telling the same story the same day more than once or telling you twice in the same conversation about what happened earlier. The more frequent the repetition the more advanced the dementia. It is easy to overlook this, but when I meet with someone and I observe this or they tell me their mom or dad repeat themselves a lot, I know that dementia is an issue no matter how much everyone protests that this is normal, it is not normal.

2. Confusion
Dementia takes away your ability to put into your brain, what happened seconds ago. The words someone said, the directions you were given never get into your brain to be processed. It is like they just bounce off. If your loved one gets confused when provided with new information this is a sign of dementia. Remember that for most people the most recent memories fail first, so it is typically only in the later stages of dementia that a person can no longer remember things from the past like who their mother was. For many as dementia advances, they are no longer able to recognize

their children often confusing them with someone else, this is a later stage so is not something to look for.

3. Getting words wrong.

My mother had several very small stokes, no one noticed them. Not my mom, her doctors or me. The thing that started to concern me was the increasing difficulty she was having finding the right word. I began worrying when she would confuse her friends' grandchildren or use my name for something my daughter said or vice versa. For the most part she seemed so alert and capable, it was hard to see this as a sign. When my mom told me she had bugs that looked like commas I wish I had seen that as a sign. (The bugs were ants) My mom tried to use kerosene to kill them but could not open the can, fortunately a neighbor was called, he spayed the ants and took away the kerosene. My mom had a more severe stroke, that caused partial aphasia (the ability to communicate) at that point her dementia was clear.

4. Making poor decisions.

There is a part of your brain called the executive function that controls our ability to make decisions. This part of the brain kicks off its development when puberty starts and is completed around age 25. It Is the last part of the brain to develop and most often the first part to be affected. The reason that "Senior Citizens" are so often the victims of scams is that they have lost part of their executive function. I describe this as a person thinking like a teenager. So just as a teen might dream of getting rich quick, so a person who has lost part of their executive function can believe they have won a lottery they did not play, that their grandson has called them from a foreign country needing money, that the IRS is calling because they owe money, that the nice person on the phone calling for a charity is really going to give the money to those in need, or that the investment in some get rich quick scheme is good. This is the most subtle form of dementia, the hardest to spot, and the reason why elder abuse is so prevalent and hard to stop.

5. Friends or Family noticing a problem.
I know we all hate our meddling relatives, the ones who come to visit and dare to say something isn't right. After all, how dare they. The reality is the closer you are to the person the less you notice the signs. You will naturally fill in the words, help them with the directions, give them a name of the person who is talking to them, you will cover for them. If you are the caregiver, you might not notice how much things have changed. If friends or family tell you they think your loved one has dementia, you should listen. The friend or family member who comes to visit will see the changes, if they are concerned enough to mention that there is a problem don't put your head in the sand, this is a clear sign something is terribly wrong.

What does Dementia or Alzheimer's really look like?

The movie "Still Alice" has a scene where Alice who has recently seen a doctor for her unexplained problems teaching her classes, getting lost etc. Her family has not yet noticed that she is having issues remembering things as she has come up with many ways to compensate. It is a holiday dinner, and her daughter brings her boyfriend. The boyfriend is introduced to Alice, she holds a pleasant conversation with him, then goes into the kitchen and when she is serving food asks him if they have met. He looks confused and introduces himself saying we just met earlier, she excuses her lapse claiming she is tired from all the cooking. The rest of the evening is uneventful, later the family recalls this when they hear the diagnosis. This scene is a good example of what the early stages of Alzheimer's or Dementia look like.

In my workshops I talk about my mother in-law Doris at her husband Paul's funeral. At this point she has been diagnosed with dementia and is under a Conservatorship. After the service her friends are greeting her as they exit the church. She can remember most of their faces, and she knows to ask about their families and children. As she talks to each old friend, I can tell they don't really think she has dementia. (I was guilty of making sure she was able to look as good as she could). However, each time there was a gap in the line she turned to me and asked, "Where is Paul?" as she looked towards the restrooms. I told her he was in heaven with Jesus, and as the next person came by, she smiled and asked about their families and children, and again as a gap occurred "Where is Paul", my answer was the same. I use this because I want people to know how easy it is for someone to fool others. Social graces are learned early in life and last well past the ability to truly remember anything.

Alzheimer's, Health Care Directives and End of Life

Alzheimer's (and other Dementia's) take away life while you are living. For those who watch their loved one fade slowly away it is truly a long goodbye. I spent the last week with my mother in-law as her life ended. As the family gathered to say goodbye, everyone said they had really grieved her loss for years, as it had been at least a year and a half since she had even a glimmer of recognizing my husband or his sister, my brother in-law and his wife had become the people who came by to give her a hug. The only thing that gave her any pleasure was listening to the hymns she loved. In the last week the decision to stop antibiotics was made and the doctor said artificial hydration was causing her distress as her body was retaining fluids. Comfort measures were put in place because that is what she wanted as stated on her health care directive. I know my mother in-law would have wanted nature to take its course, she did not want Alzheimer's as she had watched her mother die from the disease, we had kept her happy and healthy for 8 years and her mind was almost gone, she would never get better. We knew she would not want us to do everything we could to keep her alive, she believed in heaven, and we knew she wanted to join her husband there. I am glad she told us what she wanted.

The conversation about what you want is the most important conversation you can have with your children. I do know that very few people wish to be kept alive on machines, when they no longer are able to recognize the people they love, or no longer able to eat or drink on their own, especially when there is no hope that they will ever get better. As an Elder Law Attorney, I frequently am called by my client's children who want me to tell them what their mom or dad wanted. I know these calls will come so I have my client's permission to talk to their children so I can remind them about what their mom or dad said to me when they signed their Health Care Directive. It is hard to say don't give my mom food "comfort measures only" but when that is what your loved one wants it is the right decision and the end will be peaceful. I hope for all that when the day comes for you to decide for a loved one you know what they want, and you can look at an Advance Care Directive that clearly states what your loved one would want you to do and have the peace of knowing you did the right thing.

When Mom Demands to Go Home How Do You Cope

I moved my mom to a facility because she needed help with bathing, dressing, walking, eating, medication management after her health deteriorated and she showed more memory impairment after an incident which was most likely a stroke. At first, she knew she needed to be in the home, but as her health improved slightly and she was able to walk (albeit very slowly stumbling often and needing assistance) she started asking when she was coming home. At first it was easy to redirect the conversation, but as the days went by, she started to become more and more adamant that she wanted to go home.

Her complaints about the facility were all dealt with, and everyone agreed to do things the way my mom wanted. My mom had a solution she was going to go home and if she needed anything she would call her neighbors, she was sure they would be available even in the middle of the night. Her ability to communicate her needs was limited and there were times when it was impossible to figure out what she wanted. Her ability to communicate was at its worst when she was tired which meant in the middle of the night, she might not be able to communicate, sadly she did not understand how her stroke had affected her.

No amount of explaining satisfied my mother. The Doctors did not know what they were talking about, I was "Nuts" if I thought she needed someone to take care of her. "I am 91 years old, I can take care of myself". When I left after a long argument her final response was to tell me to leave, when I said I was sorry she was not able to go home because it was not safe, she said "whatever". She demanded to talk to the doctor. I contacted the hospice team and was extremely nervous about the meeting, fearful that he might tell her she could go home. I was upset the whole weekend. I knew she would not be safe at home, yet waiting for the meeting made me nervous.

Monday, I met with the nurse and Social Worker who were going to start the assessment for the doctor. I was a wreck. I had helped many people through these decisions and told them they could trust the professionals to see the deficits, yet I could only see my mother as the competent woman she had been. I had seen her memory loss, yet she compensated so well prior to her stroke she had managed to live alone despite her deficits relying on neighbors and the caregivers who came 4 hours a day three days a week so I had deceived myself into believing she was okay so now when she wasn't I worried that she could still convince me and the professionals that she could care for herself.

I was no longer a little girl who had to do what her mother said, I was an adult who needed to make decisions for my mother. I needed support we all do. My mother did not accept the fact that she could not go home. Yet, knowing I was making the right decision and making sure my mom received the best care possible comforted me. I knew I had to make the right decision, and that my mom could not go home. It helped to have the support of the social worker, nurse and doctor.

I turned to my Elder Law Attorney friends, because like me they have helped others along the path, I also literally told myself what I told my clients. It was during this time I truly committed myself to making sure that my law practice would always be different, to make sure I was available to my clients to support them during the difficult decisions.

Chapter 2: Three Important Things You Need to Know About Planning for Someone with Dementia

Dementia is a disease that takes a person away from the ones they love while they are alive. It takes a financial and emotional toil. The signs of dementia at the beginning are subtle, forgetting names, or doing things that are out of character. If you suspect a loved one has dementia you should have them consult a Neurologist. If your loved one is not willing to get diagnosed, you are wise to start planning.

My mother in-law has dementia, and now barely recognizes her children, but it was not that long ago everyone was wondering if she had dementia. If my father in-law had discussed his concerns with their attorney (or with his daughter in-law Martha Patterson an Elder Law Attorney), the disaster that resulted in Probate Court proceedings could have been avoided.

Here Are Three Things You Need to Know:

1. If Your Loved One Has Dementia a Traditional Plan Can Fail
   Traditional Estate Plans (Wills and Trusts) are designed for what happens when you die and not what happens if you live with

Dementia. A family with a loved one with dementia needs a plan that plans for eligibility for public benefits such as Medi-Cal and Veteran's Benefits, and a plan that makes sure that a person who can take care of everything involved with the day to day care needs of a loved one with dementia, and a plan that makes it easy for someone to step in if a loved one is unable to make rational decisions.

2. Denying Dementia Does Not Make It Go Away

It is really easy for families to deny the reality of dementia. People with dementia are able to remember details of past events and are able to fake that they know what is going on. Don't be fooled. If you are asking if it is dementia, it most likely is. Don't be deceived by a diagnosis of "mild cognitive impairment" a mild impairment is serious and will get worse. Don't wait, talk to an Elder Law Attorney and get your loved one to a physician who can diagnose your loved one and provide medications that can make the symptoms less severe.

3. You Will Need Help Caring for Your Loved One

   80% of caregivers die before the person with dementia. My father in-law was one of them. My mother in-law was not sleeping, and he had not told anyone he was not getting rest. Sundowner's is common leaving the caregiver exhausted. The toll of caring for someone with dementia is impossible to understate, the caregiver's day is the equivalent of a working 3 jobs with no breaks. Help is necessary and expensive and though Geisler Patterson Law is able to help people get help from Medi-Cal or though Veteran's Benefits, these benefits require planning and compromise as they often do not cover the care a family really wants for a loved one, and there is very little help available to keep a loved one at home.

How to Protect Your Parent and Preserve Their Dignity

When my mom turned 91 and her health had been failing for a long time. At that time both her mind and body were failing. She was a sucker for the "nice man" and has been taken advantage of by repair men who overcharged her. My mom gets tons of mail, most of it solicitations. Of course she gets people calling her to sell her stuff too. My mother was fiercely independent and managed her home and finances alone since my dad passed 41 years ago.

A well drafted Trust combined with well drafted Powers of Attorney for Finances and Health Care provided her a lot of protection. The well drafted Trust and Powers of Attorney for Finances and Health Care had every provision needed to enable me to take over when she can no longer do so, and that I hopefully will never need to go to court. I know that even with the best planning that a loved one as fiercely independent as my mother can get angry and change all the great planning requiring the loving family to go to court. However, there are ways to

Removing a Trustee with Dementia "the Escape Clause"

In California most people have living Trusts and the people who created the Trust are the Trustees. This works well allowing people to avoid probate when they die but to live like they would if they had not created a Trust. A Trust is a contract to hold property and describes what happens when you die and also most Trusts describe what happens if the person who created the Trust becomes incapacitated.

Most people don't want the Courts involved, most people want to make it easy to remove a Trustee since most people understand that if you lose your ability to make good decisions you want to make it easy for your spouse or the person you Trust to take over.

Martha Patterson is passionate about making it as simple as possible for families to remove someone with dementia, since she knows firsthand how difficult it can be when you can't get a loved one to go to a doctor to have them declared incapacitated. It is good that the Courts are there to protect someone from a wrongful declaration of incapacity and it is good that most families can avoid going to court by planning easier ways than getting two doctors. The decision of how you are removed as Trustee is something you should discuss with your attorney.

Chapter 3: Conservatorships and Protecting Your Parents

What is a Conservatorship?

A conservatorship is when a judge appoints another person to act of make decisions for the person who needs help. The person the Judge appoints is called the Conservator. The person who needs help is the Conservatee.

A Conservator is the only person who can make decisions for another, decisions they don't agree with. ONLY a Conservator can place someone in a Memory Care Unit without their consent. ONLY a Conservator can void a contract signed by their loved one.

A person is presumed competent unless they are under a Conservatorship so the only way to stop them from giving money away to bad guys is to obtain a Conservatorship.

Conservatorships take away all the legal rights you obtain when you turn 18, so they require a lot of proof. The court requires you to account for every penny of the Conservators money, and they find out about all the things you don't want anyone to know. They are invasive. They are EXPENSIVE. Sadly, there is also corruption in the system so the court can take over and cause an estate to lose money due to actions of a professional fiduciary, or court appointed attorney.

Lessons from the Casey Kasem case

I was quoted on ABC, CBS, NBC, Good Morning America and other media sources as saying, "Isolation is the most common form of abuse".   I don't think my other statement "family members are the most common abusers" was quoted. Sadly, as a Certified Elder Law Attorney I hear about Elder Abuse too often. The stories are similar, typically someone in the family is "helping", and the parent is increasingly dependent on their spouse or child, the "helper" takes over rarely if ever allowing others to see the venerable elder, and as time goes on the "helper" makes sure their name is on bank accounts, stock accounts and even real property, and of course the elders money is used to buy things for the "helper". This process can take years or days. Meanwhile the other family members worry; they try to see their loved one and are often prevented from doing so.

Sadly, when a person suspects their parent is being abused, they are almost always right. If you suspect elder abuse, you need to take action.

Conservatorships are the best option for protecting a vulnerable adult. In Los Angeles County your loved one will have an attorney appointed for them. The attorney is to be an advocate and the eyes and ears of the court. As an attorney on the PVP Panel I know that those who have volunteered take their jobs seriously, and make sure their clients have a voice in what happens and in who is appointed to care for them.

Casey Kasem tried to plan for his incapacity. He signed a healthcare directive naming his daughter Julie and her husband Jamil as his first choice of people to make decisions if he was no longer able, then if Julie and Jamil could not serve, he named his daughter Kerri and then his son Mike. In 2011 new documents were prepared naming Jean Kasem as the person to make those decisions. Like many families where there are signs of elder abuse there are competing Advance Health Care Directives and Powers of Attorney.

In the Casey Kasem case, the court has suspended the Advance Health Care directive held by Jean Kasem. It is important to have solid legal documents, and also to use the courts when needed as even bad people can get legal document.

Chapter 4: Coping with Dementia

When Mom Demands to Go Home How Do You Cope

I moved my mom to a facility because she needed help with bathing, dressing, walking, eating, medication management after her health deteriorated and she showed more memory impairment after an incident which was most likely a stroke. At first, she knew she needed to be in the home, but as her health improved slightly and she was able to walk (albeit very slowly stumbling often and needing assistance) she started asking when she was coming home. At first it was easy to redirect the conversation, but as the days went by, she started to become more and more adamant that she wanted to go home.

Her complaints about the facility were all dealt with, and everyone agreed to do things the way my mom wanted. My mom had a solution she was going to go home and if she needed anything she would call her neighbors, she was sure they would be available even in the middle of the night. Her ability to communicate her needs was limited and there were times when it was impossible to figure out what she wanted. Her ability to communicate was at its worst when she was tired which meant in the middle of the night, she might not be able to communicate, sadly she did not understand how her stroke had affected her.

No amount of explaining satisfied my mother. The Doctors did not know what they were talking about, I was "Nuts" if I thought she needed someone to take care of her. "I am 91 years old, I can take care of myself". When I left after a long argument her final response was to tell me to leave, when I said I was sorry she was not able to go home because it was not safe, she said "whatever". She demanded to talk to the doctor. I contacted the hospice team and was extremely nervous about the meeting, fearful that he might tell her she could go home. I was upset the whole weekend. I knew she would not be safe at home, yet waiting for the meeting made me nervous.

Monday, I met with the nurse and Social Worker who were going to start the assessment for the doctor. I was a wreck. I had helped many people through these decisions and told them they could trust the professionals to see the deficits, yet I could only see my mother as the competent woman she had been. I had seen her memory loss, yet she compensated so well prior to her stroke she had managed to live alone despite her deficits relying on neighbors and the caregivers who came 4 hours a day three days a week so I had deceived myself into believing she was okay so now when she wasn't I worried that she could still convince me and the professionals that she could care for herself.

I was no longer a little girl who had to do what her mother said, I was an adult who needed to make decisions for my mother. I needed support we all do. My mother did not accept the fact that she could not go home. Yet, knowing I was making the right decision and making sure my mom received the best care possible comforted me. I knew I had to make the right decision, and that my mom could not go home. It helped to have the support of the social worker, nurse and doctor. I turned to my Elder Law Attorney friends, because like me they have helped others along the path, I also literally told myself what I told my clients. It was during this time I truly committed myself to making sure that my law practice would always be different, to make sure I was available to my clients to support them during the difficult decisions.

How to Protect Your Parent and Preserve Their Dignity

When my mom turned 91 and her health had been failing for a long time. At that time both her mind and body were failing. She was a sucker for the "nice man" and has been taken advantage of by repair men who overcharged her. My mom gets tons of mail, most of its solicitations. Of course she gets people calling her to sell her stuff too. My mother was fiercely independent and managed her home and finances alone since my dad passed 41 years ago.

A well drafted Trust combined with well drafted Powers of Attorney for Finances and Health Care provided her a lot of protection. The well drafted Trust and Powers of Attorney for Finances and Health Care had every provision needed to enable me to take over when she can no longer do so, and that I hopefully will never need to go to court. I know that even with the best planning that a loved one as fiercely independent as my mother can get angry and change all the great planning requiring the loving family to go to court. However, there are ways to

Removing a Trustee with Dementia "the Escape Clause"

In California most people have living Trusts and the people who created the Trust are the Trustees. This works well allowing people to avoid probate when they die but to live like they would if they had not created a Trust. A Trust is a contract to hold property and describes what happens when you die and also most Trusts describe what happens if the person who created the Trust becomes incapacitated.

Most people don't want the Courts involved, most people want to make it easy to remove a Trustee since most people understand that if you lose your ability to make good decisions you want to make it easy for your spouse or the person you Trust to take over.

Martha Patterson is passionate about making it as simple as possible for families to remove someone with dementia, since she knows firsthand how difficult it can be when you can't get a loved one to go to a doctor to have them declared incapacitated. It is good that the Courts are there to protect someone from a wrongful declaration of incapacity and it is good that most families can avoid going to court by planning easier ways than getting two doctors. The decision of how you are removed as Trustee is something you should discuss with your attorney.

Ten Absolutes with Dementia

1. Never <u>ARGUE</u>, Instead <u>AGREE</u>.
2. Never <u>REASON</u>, Instead <u>DIVERT</u>.
3. Never <u>SHAME</u>, Instead <u>DISTRACT</u>.
4. Never <u>LECTURE</u>, Instead <u>REASSURE</u>.
5. Never Say <u>REMEMBER</u>, Instead Say <u>REMINISCE</u>.
6. Never Say <u>I TOLD YOU</u>, Instead <u>REPEAT</u>.
7. Never Say <u>YOU CAN'T</u>, Instead Say <u>DO WHAT YOU CAN</u>.
8. Never <u>COMMAND</u> Or <u>DEMAND</u>, Instead <u>ASK</u> Or <u>MODEL</u>.
9. Never <u>CONDESCEND</u>, Instead <u>ENCOURAGE</u> And <u>PRAISE</u>.
10. Never <u>FORCE</u>, Instead <u>REINFORCE</u>.

Chapter 5: Placing Your Loved One in a Home

Placing your loved one in a facility is never easy. I have placed my mother in-law, my mom, my husband and my Aunt Carol. Why? Home care is too expensive. As I write this book rates for home care are $35.00 to $50.00 an hour through an agency. A home care worker is your employee. You are required to follow all wage and hour rules, including breaks, lunch and wages. The Cost if you do it yourself is about $28.00 an hour after you pay taxes and Worker's Compensation Insurance (required).

In addition to the cost the reasons for placing each family member were different. My mom was falling and after her stroke, she needed assistance, my mother in-law was wandering out of her home looking for my father in-law, for my husband I could no longer work and take care of him, Aunt Carol lived alone and has no family other than her nieces and nephews and she was no longer safe at home.

Families struggle with this decision as they often have promised their loved one, they would never place them. I understand wanting to keep that promise. Unfortunately, not every promise should be kept. A spouse should not literally kill themselves taking care of their loved one. No family member should endure physical, verbal or emotional abuse caring for a loved one. Families should not go broke caring for a person at home, and it is okay to choose the less expensive options.

Most people must privately pay for home care and for care in a facility. The Medi-Cal program for Home Care: In Home Supportive Services is only available to people with low income and Medicare does not pay for Caregivers in your home. Medi-Cal pays for Skilled Nursing Facilities regardless of income, however, to get into a Skilled Nursing Home, you need to have a medical reason for admission. There is a Medi-Cal program that pays for Assisted Living. The Assisted Living Waiver program has very few spots available (17,000 in 2024) and is only available for people with a very low income, as you must qualify for NO Share of Cost Medi-Cal to get a spot.

Chapter 6: Kinds of Facilities for Long term Care

What is Residential Care for the Elderly?

Residential Care Facilities for the Elderly (RCFEs) — sometimes called "Assisted Living" (e.g., 16+ beds) or "Board and Care" (e.g., 4 to 16 beds) — are non–medical facilities that provide room, meals, housekeeping, supervision, storage and distribution of medication, and personal care assistance with basic activities like hygiene, dressing, eating, bathing and transferring. Residential Care Facilities for the Elderly serve persons 60 years of age and older.

This level of care and supervision is for people who are unable to live by themselves but who do not need 24-hour nursing care. They are considered non-medical facilities and are not required to have nurses, certified nursing assistants or doctors on staff.

How Does a Residential Care Facility for the Elderly Differ from an Assisted Living Facility?

From a licensing standpoint, there is no difference. In California, facilities describing themselves as assisted living and offering personal care and supervision are licensed as Residential Care Facilities for the Elderly.

Residential Care Facilities for the Elderly are dominated by smaller (i.e., 6 to 15 beds), locally owned facilities with shared rooms. Larger facilities usually offer private apartments and tend to be corporately owned. Many larger facilities have different fee options depending on the type of care needed.

Residential Care Facilities for the Elderly or Assisted Living Facilities must meet care and safety standards set by the State and are licensed and inspected by the Department of Social Services, Community Care Licensing (CCL). They are also subject to all local fire and building and safety codes

Senior housing complexes, retirement villages or retirement hotels that provide only housing, housekeeping and meals are not required to be licensed as Residential Care Facilities for the Elderly. The key feature is that they provide NO personal care or supervision.

Some Residential Care Facility for the Elderly offer special services to persons with dementia if they meet certain licensing requirements. Make sure that the facility has experience in providing dementia care and meets all of the state licensing standards to provide dementia care.

Some Residential Care Facility for the Elderly also accept or retain someone with Medical Care Needs; however, it will depend on the type and severity of the medical condition(s) and whether the facility meets the state licensing standards for restrictive health conditions. Some medical conditions are not allowed in a Residential Care Facility for the Elderly (e.g., tube feeding, or treatment of open bedsores). Check the facility's license to see if it has met the requirements to serve persons who need help in leaving the building in case of emergency (i.e., non-ambulatory) or with certain medical conditions (e.g., hospice waiver).

If your loved one's medical needs increase, they may or may not be able to stay, as a RCFE is not licensed as a "medical" facility, persons requiring tube feeding, treatment of open bedsores or in need of 24-hour nursing care are not permitted to reside in RCFEs. However, some RCFEs have permission to care for persons on hospice.

The administrators of these facilities must take a 40–hour certification program, pass a simple state exam, and obtain 40 hours of continuing education every two years. They must be 21 years of age and possess a high school diploma or equivalent for facilities of 15 beds or less — these comprise over 80% of all RCFEs. For facilities of 16 to 49 beds, the administrator needs 15 college credits; and for facilities of 50+ beds, 2 years of college or 3 years' experience, or equivalent education and experience.

Staff must be 18 years of age and pass the criminal background check; as well as receive at least 10 hours of training at the facility within 4 weeks of employment, and at least 4 hours annually thereafter. For facilities advertising dementia care, 6 hours of orientation specific to dementia care within the first 4 weeks, and at least 8 hours annually of in–service training.

Please note because RCFEs are non–medical facilities, there is no requirement for RNs, LVNs or CNAs or any medically trained personnel. Check on the qualifications of the administrator and key staff.

There is no specific staff to resident ratio for assisted living/residential care facilities. Regulations state that facility personnel shall at all times be sufficient in numbers and competency to provide the services necessary to meet resident needs. (CCR, Title 22, Section 87411.) In regard to night supervision, for facilities with 15 or fewer residents, there has to be one "qualified" person on call and on the premises; in facilities with 16–100 residents, there shall be one person awake and, on the premises, and another on call and capable of responding within 10 minutes. (CCR, Title 22, Section 87415.)

The cost for these facilities will depend on a variety of factors such as the type of accommodations (e.g., apartment, private room, or shared room), the range of services needed, and the geographic area. The average monthly cost in California is from $2,500 to $3,000, with costs ranging from a low of around $1,000 a month for a resident on Supplemental Security Income (SSI) to over $5,000 a month. Specialized services like dementia or hospice care are more costly.

Since residential care is a private business, providers will charge what the market will bear. However, facilities must issue 60–day notices to increase rates but can raise charges for level of care changes immediately and provide notice within 2 working days

Facilities can charge a pre–admission fee; with some providers charging nothing or a minimum amount to cover costs of conducting an assessment, obtaining medical records and setting up files, where others charge fees of thousands of dollars. It is important to demand a written description of what the fees cover. Negotiate the amount if too high or look for another facility. Facilities are prohibited from charging security deposits.

Most people must pay privately for care. Long-term care insurance only covers a very small percentage of people. There is very limited public funding through Supplemental Security Income (SSI) for RCFE residents who qualify for this program, unfortunately, the SSI rate is so low that fewer and fewer facilities will accept persons on SSI. Aid and Attendance is a benefit paid by Veterans Affairs (VA) to veterans, veteran spouses or surviving spouses that may help pay for residential care.

Because these are not medical facilities, neither Medicare nor Medi–Cal pays directly for the residential care/assisted living.

If you desire to know the track record of a given facility, you may (and should) request it. Upon request, a facility must show you the most recent copy of its latest inspection report (Note: Inspections are only required every five years, and annually if the facility is in non–compliance); and a copy of any substantiated complaints within the past year. The regulatory agency does not post compliance information on its web site, nor does it make such information available electronically to organizations like CANHR. The only way to view the record to is go to one of the district offices of Community Care Licensing and request to view the public record of the facility.

You also can contact the local District Office of Community Care Licensing to receive a listing of facilities. Some Ombudsman Programs also have listings, offer pre-placement services, and provide access to licensing reports

What is a Nursing Home in California?

All nursing homes in California must be licensed by the California Department of Public Health (DPH) and meet California nursing home standards.

In addition to being licensed, nursing homes that choose to participate in the Medicare and Medi–Cal programs must be certified by the federal government in order to qualify for payments from these programs. Federally certified facilities must meet federal standards as well as the California requirements. Most California nursing homes are certified to participate in both Medicare and Medi–Cal.

All nursing homes are not alike. There are several types of licensing and certification categories for nursing homes, which are described below:

Most nursing homes in California are licensed as Skilled Nursing Facilities (SNFs), which California broadly defines as a health facility that provides skilled nursing and supportive care to persons who need this type of care on an extended basis.

Medicare also uses the term "skilled nursing facility" for nursing homes that are certified to receive its payments. Medi–Cal uses a similar term, "nursing facility (NF)", for nursing homes that are certified to receive Medi–Cal payments. Most, but not all, licensed skilled nursing facilities in California are certified to participate in Medicare and Medi–Cal.

Distinct Part/Skilled Nursing Facility (DP/SNF) is a hospital–based facility, usually operated in a designated unit within a hospital. These facilities are paid higher Medi–Cal rates than freestanding nursing homes.

Medi–Cal contracts with certain skilled nursing facilities to provide sub-acute care to adults and children who need specialized care. Sub-acute care is a Medi–Cal program (not a licensing or certification category) that pays higher rates for Medi–Cal beneficiaries who have exceptional needs, such as ventilator care.

Intermediate Care Facilities (ICFs) are a lower level of nursing home licensed by the California Department of Public Health to provide inpatient care to persons who do not require continuous nursing care but do need nursing supervision and supportive care. Most ICFs are certified by Medi–Cal and qualify for its payments, although at a lower rate than skilled nursing facilities. Medicare does not certify or pay ICFs, although Medicare beneficiaries who reside in ICFs can use Medicare for covered health services, such as physician care.

Some nursing homes, classified as Institutes for Mental Disease (IMDs), provide care for residents with mental health disorders. In California, these skilled nursing facilities are designated as special treatment programs (SNF/STPs).

Ask to see the entire facility, not just the nicely decorated lobby and one wing or floor. Remember that appearances can be deceptive. Though environment is important, try to get a feel for the care provided and how the residents are treated by staff.

Making the transition to a Care Facility: Practical Tips

The decision to consider placement in a long-term care facility such as a residential care facility for the elderly (sometimes called assisted living) or a nursing home is a complex and emotionally demanding process. Pre-planning and the involvement of the person entering a care facility will help ease the transition. Unfortunately, there is limited or no planning for many placement decisions. Most people end up being forced to move when a fall, an illness, the death of their caregiver or other incident makes living at home no longer possible.

My mother in-law has dementia, and we had to place her in a Secured Alzheimer's facility for her safety; because when her husband was hospitalized, she was unable to cope. In my Alzheimer's Resource Kit (for your FREE copy www.AlzheimersAnswersNow.com), my friend Jo

Huey talks about the brain gizmo being broken. That is a good description of dementia and Alzheimer's. My mother in-law believed she could care for herself, a late-night visit to the neighbors looking for her husband, a metal pan in the microwave, food left uneaten out to spoil, all showed us she could not take care of herself. It was the hardest thing my husband and his brother ever did was to obtain court permission and then force their mom to leave her home and live somewhere else.

Even in the best of circumstances there will be strong feelings of loss and abandonment by the person being placed and guilt by the person assuming responsibility for the placement. Acknowledging these feelings is one way to cope with the transition.

Visiting frequently can also be helpful. During some of these visits, if possible, try to meet other residents, talk to staff and explore other parts of the facility in an effort to familiarize yourself and your loved one to his/her new environment.

There are some other very practical things that can be done during the transition:

• Make sure that he/she is given a comprehensive assessment. If he/she is being discharged from the hospital, make sure they are checked for skin breakdown and possible over-medication.

• Become involved in the care planning process right away. You know your loved one the best. Assist the facility in getting to know them and work with the staff in developing a transitional care plan and then a more comprehensive one.

• Monitor their needs, changes and care during the transition. They might experience depression that will affect their appetite, sleeping patterns, motivation, and ability to socialize and to participate in therapy or activities. A new environment, a roommate, or different medications can also affect a person. Be attentive to changes and communicate them to the appropriate staff.

• When asked when they can come home if they are mentally sound deal with the physical reality and be open and honest. If their memory is fading remember home is not the place where they were just living it is in their mind the place where they lived when their memory was good. Jo Huey provides a good response, "So do I", we all want to go to that place where life was happy, and our loved one could remember and take care of themselves.

Chapter 7: Hard questions to ask before selecting a Nursing home

No question is unreasonable to ask when selection a facility for a loved one. You are paying a large amount of money for the care of your loved one; reticence on the part of staff to answer questions is not a good sign, as things seldom get better than at the beginning. Photocopy these questions and clipboard them before going to a facility, it makes comparing so much easier.

Questions to ask about Staff

•	Are there adequate staff? What is the staff to resident ratio? Are call bells and resident requests responded to in a timely manner (5 minutes or so)?

•	Are the staff courteous to residents? Do they treat residents with dignity and respect? Or is the staff attitude condescending? Are childish or otherwise inappropriate nicknames used when speaking with residents? Do staff talk about residents as if they were not present or as if they were children?

•	Does the administrator/manager and director of nurses appear to know the residents?

- Is the administrator friendly and receptive to questions?

- Is privacy respected (e.g., knocking on doors before entering rooms, keeping privacy curtains drawn while care is being given)?

- Does staff wear nametags?

- Are there therapists on staff or does the facility contract out for therapy?

- Is there a licensed social worker on staff? Full time?

- Does the facility have permanent full–time nurses and certified nurse assistants (CNA's) or are registry nurses and aides used?

- Are the staff visible and actively assisting residents?

- In addition to English, what languages does the staff speak?

- What is the facility's communication strategy when a resident's first language is not English?

- Does the facility conduct background checks before hiring staff?

Resident Appearance

- Are residents up and dressed for breakfast? Does the staff get them up hours before breakfast (too early) or just before lunch (too late)?

- Are the residents well–groomed (shaved, clothes clean, hair combed, nails trimmed and clean)?

- Do residents appear alert, content and occupied? Or are they lethargic, listless or stuporous?

- Are residents comfortably positioned in comfortable chairs? Are they restrained in their chairs or beds? Are they in chairs that have a tray or "lap buddy?"

Questions to ask about Resident Rooms

- In which area of the facility would the resident's room be located?

- How many residents share a room? Generally, rooms should have no more than four beds, at least three feet apart, with privacy curtains around each bed.

- Does each bedroom have a window?

- Is there a bedside stand, reading light, chest of drawers, and at least one comfortable chair for each resident? Is there adequate storage space and is it separate from other roommates?

•   Are the beds easy to reach? Is there room to maneuver a wheelchair or Geri Chair easily?

•   Are call buttons accessible to residents?

•   Is there fresh drinking water at the bedside?

•   Are residents allowed and encouraged to bring any of their own belongings or furniture? Have residents personalized their rooms?

Facility Environment

•   Is there an obvious odor in the facility? Strong urine and body odors may indicate poor nursing care or poor housekeeping. Heavy "air freshener", deodorants, and other temporary chemical cover–ups may be substitutes for conscientious care and maintenance.

•   Is the facility maintained at a comfortable temperature? Do the rooms have heating, air conditioning, and individual thermostats?

•   Is the facility clean, well–lit and free of hazards? Do you see soiled linen or is it properly disposed of? Is there adequate linen?

•   Is furniture sturdy and comfortable?

•   Are floors clean and non-slippery?

Hallways, Stairs and Lounges

- Are halls free of obstacles and debris?

- Are stairways and exits clearly marked?

- Are there handrails in all corridors?

- Are fire extinguishers visible? Is there a disaster plan posted and does the facility have drills?

- How many lounge areas are available for residents and visitors? Are they clean and comfortably furnished? Is there sufficient room for visiting?

Bath and Shower Rooms

*   Are bathrooms conveniently located?

*   How many residents share a bathroom?

*   Do bathrooms have handgrips or rails near all toilet and bathing areas?

*   Is there a call button near the toilet?

*   Do residents have a choice between a shower or bath, how frequent and during which shift?

Kitchen and Dining Areas

*   Is the kitchen clean and well organized?

*   Is the food handled and stored in a safe and sanitary manner?

*   Is the dining area pleasant, clean and comfortable?

*   How many residents eat in the dining area? Is it large enough to accommodate most of the residents? Are there shifts for meals?

*   Do chairs fit under the table so that residents are comfortably close to their food?

Menus and Food

Try to visit the facility during a meal. Observe the way the food is served, how residents are assisted with eating and what their reaction is to the food. You can probably buy a meal to sample the food.

• A menu for the current and following week should be posted. If a menu is not posted, ask to see one. Is the food listed on the menu actually being served?

• How often are meals repeated? Are alternatives available, as required by law?

• Does the food appear and smell appetizing? Is it nutritious? Are fresh foods used, or is it mostly canned or frozen? Do residents enjoy the food?

• Are dishes and silverware used, or are disposable plates and utensils used?

• Are those residents who need assistance with eating and who are being fed by nurse's aides finishing their meals and eating at their own pace? Are assistive devices available to those who may be able to feed themselves with a little help?

• Are meals served at appropriate temperatures?

• What provisions are made for patients who are unable to eat in the dining room?

• Who plans the meals? Is a professional dietician on staff? How are special dietary needs met?

Activities

• Are activity calendars posted? If not, ask for a description of the activity program. Meet the Activity Director if possible.

• Do the activities cover a broad range of interests?

• Are activities tailored to individual preferences?

• Does the facility have outside areas for resident use? Do staff assist the residents in using these areas?

• What activities are available to residents confined to their rooms?

• Do volunteers visit the facility?

• What arrangements are made for residents to participate in religious services of their choice?

• What is done for holidays and birthdays?

• Is there a resident council? When does it meet and what is its function?

Miscellaneous

- Is there a Family Council? When does it meet and who are the officers?

- How often do residents' physicians visit the facility? It should be at least once every 30 days.

- How long has the facility been operating under the present management? Are there any plans to change in the near future?

- What hospital is used in emergencies?

- What is the billing procedure?

- Who should be contacted when there is a problem?

- How does the facility notify the resident and family members of the time and place of the quarterly care planning meetings?

- Is the Ombudsman Program's phone number posted?

- Are the results from the last inspection by the Department of Public Health posted?

- Ask to review a copy of the admission agreement. Does the facility demand a "responsible party" signature? What is their "informed consent" policy?

- What is included in the basic costs and what is extra?

- If you are looking at an Alzheimer's Unit within a facility, what makes it different from the rest of the facility (especially if it costs more)?

- How is transportation provided for trips to hospitals, medical offices, or community functions? Is there a charge?

- How is personal laundry handled?

- Is there a system to protect wanderers? Is it operational? Ask for a demonstration.

OTHER CONSIDERATIONS IN SELECTING A FACILITY

Medicare and Medi–Cal Considerations

- If you want Medicare or Medi–Cal to help pay for the nursing home care, you must select a facility that is certified by these programs. Due to the extremely high cost of nursing home care – which averages above $200 per day or $7,549 per month – few people can afford to pay privately for very long. Most California nursing homes participate in both Medicare and Medi–Cal.

- Medicare's short–term skilled nursing facility benefit is very limited but is often helpful to gain admission to a nursing home, especially when skilled nursing care or therapy are needed after hospitalization due to a stroke, surgery, injury or other medical conditions. Medicare covers up to 100 days of skilled nursing care following a hospital stay of at least three days.

• Medi–Cal helps pay nursing home care for two–of–every–three residents in California. Due to the high cost of nursing home care, most people in nursing home's will meet Medi–Cal's financial eligibility requirements sometime during their stay. Even if you don't need or qualify for Medi–Cal now, it is best to select a Medi–Cal certified facility. Uncertified facilities can evict you when your money and insurance runs out. Your choice of other facilities at that point may be very limited. Medi–Cal certified facilities cannot evict residents who qualify for Medi–Cal during their stay.

• Although it is illegal for a certified nursing home to require a resident to pay privately for any set period of time, many nursing homes give preference to applicants who can pay privately. The longer you can pay the private rate, the more options you will have when looking for a facility.

Location

• It is important to select a nursing home that is close and convenient to the person(s) who will be visiting the resident most often. Residents who have frequent visitors often recover faster, are happier and healthier from the love and attention received and tend to receive a higher quality of care. When family members and friends are close enough to visit frequently, they can monitor the resident's condition, participate in care planning and respond quickly to emergencies.

Special Needs

•   Always seek a nursing home that can meet any special care needs your loved one may have. For example, some residents need specialized respiratory care, such as a ventilator, that is only available at certain facilities. Or an individual may need extra supervision and assistance due to behaviors associated with dementia. Ask detailed questions to make sure facilities under consideration are currently able to provide the necessary care.

Seek References

•   If possible, seek information about facilities under consideration from people you trust. Relatives, friends, clergy, local senior groups, ombudsman programs, Alzheimer's support groups, hospital discharge planners, doctors and others may have recent experiences with nursing homes in your area. You can also seek opinions from residents and visitors while making visits to check on nursing homes.

Personal Visits

• Nothing substitutes for a personal visit to the facility. Once you have identified a nursing home that seems (on paper, at least) to be affordable, to have the services necessary and to have a vacancy, visit the facility. Take your clipboard of questions from this book with you. Ask to see the entire facility, not just the nicely decorated lobby or a designated unit. Try to get a feel for the quality of care and how residents are treated by the staff. Resident appearance, use of restraints, residents' rooms, quality of food and activities are all– important factors in evaluating a nursing home. However, nothing is more important than the quality and quantity of nursing home staff.

• How do you feel when you visit the facility? How does it compare to others? How did the administrator and staff treat you? Remember that you'll be depending on these people to take care of your loved one. If you don't like visiting there, imagine what it would be like living there.

- People sometimes over–estimate the importance of an attractive building. While a nursing home should be safe, clean and comfortable, it doesn't do the potential resident any good to choose a "fancy" nursing home if the resident can't afford it, if it can't meet the resident's needs or if it is too far away for family and friends to visit.

Arranging Care During Hospitalization

- Many people are admitted to nursing homes from hospitals. If your family member or friend is hospitalized, contact the hospital's discharge planning or social work office as soon as possible to request assistance in arranging nursing home care. Hospitals are required to help patients locate and obtain care and services they will need upon discharge and cannot discharge patients to nursing homes without their consent and cannot charge for extra days of care if they have not met their discharge planning responsibilities.

Some hospitals are more helpful and cooperative than others, but all are equally responsible to give you professional, timely assistance.

Legal Assistance

Aging persons and their family members face many unique legal issues. The legal, financial, and care planning issues facing the prospective nursing home resident and family can be particularly complex. If you or a family member needs nursing home care, it is clear that you need legal help. Where can you turn for that help? It is difficult for the consumer to be able to identify lawyers who have the training and experience required to provide guidance during this most difficult time. Generally, nursing home planning and Medi-Cal planning is an aspect of the services provided by Elder Law attorneys. Consumers must be cautious in choosing a lawyer and carefully investigate the lawyer's credentials. Martha Jo Patterson devotes her practice to nursing home planning and has substantially more knowledge and experience to address the issues properly as she is a Nationally Certified Elder Law Attorney. Don't hesitate to ask the lawyer how much of their practice involves nursing home planning. An attorney should devote at least 12 hours of education annually on Elder Law in addition to other legal education. Attending these sessions takes time and commitment on the part of the lawyer and is a good sign that the lawyer is attempting to stay up to date on nursing home issues.

Chapter 8: What About Medicare?

There is a great deal of confusion about Medicare and Medicaid or Medi-Cal. Medicare is the federally funded and state administered health insurance program primarily designed for older individuals (i.e. those over age 65). There are some limited long term care benefits that can be available under Medicare. In general, if you are enrolled in the traditional Medicare plan, and you've had a hospital stay of at least three days, and then you are admitted into a skilled nursing facility (often for rehabilitation or skilled nursing care), Medicare may pay for a while. (If you are a Medicare Managed Care Plan beneficiary, a three-day hospital stay may not be required to qualify.)

If you qualify, traditional Medicare may pay the full cost of the nursing home stay for the first 20 days and can continue to pay the cost of the nursing home stay for the next 80 days, but with a deductible that's nearly $150. per day. Some Medicare supplement insurance policies will pay the cost of that deductible. For Medicare Managed Care Plan enrollees, there is no deductible for days 21 through 100, as long as the strict qualifying rules continue to be met. So, in the best-case scenario, the traditional Medicare or the Medicare Managed Care Plan may pay up to 100 days for each "spell of illness." In order to qualify for these 100 days of coverage, however, the nursing home resident must be receiving daily "skilled care" and generally must continue to "improve". (Note: Once the Medicare and Managed Care beneficiary has not received a Medicare covered level of care for 60 consecutive days, the beneficiary may again be eligible for the 100 days of skilled nursing coverage for the next spell of illness). While it is never possible to predict at the outset how long Medicare will cover the rehabilitation, from our experience it usually falls far short of the 100-day maximum. Even if Medicare does cover the 100-day period, what then? What happens after the 100 days of coverage have been used? At that point, in either case you're back to one of the other alternatives: Long term care insurance, paying the bills with your own assets, or qualifying for Medicaid.

Chapter 9: What is Estate Planning and Why is it important?

You have worked hard; you should want to protect your family. Estate Planning is giving what you have, to whom you want, the way you want with the least taxes and fees possible.

My goal is to help everyone who comes in my office to achieve that goal.

It's taken years of hard work to get where you are today. Now you want to protect your assets for your enjoyment and that of your loved ones; maintain control of your affairs should you become incapacitated; and ensure that your wishes will be carried out after you are gone. Chances are, you have a number of questions about how to accomplish these goals, including:

- What do I need to do to control my property during my lifetime?
- How can I leave the most to my children, grandchildren, and loved ones without losing control of my assets?
- How do I eliminate or minimize income, gift, estate and capital gains taxes?
- What are the best ways to protect and preserve my assets?

- What is the best way to protect my real estate investments?
- How do I protect my children and loved ones from losing their inheritances to predators, creditors, family disharmony, or even their own poor decisions?
- Will I outlive my money if I need nursing home or assisted living care?
- Do I need long term care insurance?

The answers to these and other questions can only be answered on an individual basis, by an attorney like me whose practice is concentrated on estate planning and asset protection planning as well as specializing in elder law. I hope that this book will be a tool and guide to help you along in beginning to answer some of these questions.

Estate planning isn't about how much money you have, it's about protecting what you have for you, during your lifetime and for those you love after you're gone. It ensures what you have gets to the people you love, the way you want, when you want.

If you were to die today, are you comfortable everything will be taken care of the way you wanted? Estate planning is legally ensuring things will be handled the way you want by providing sufficient instructions.

Estate Planning really is for *everyone*. It doesn't matter if you have $40,000 or $400,000. You still must plan for the future. Whether it's to name a guardian for your minor children or ensure your children don't blow through your assets if you unexpectedly die or become disabled (Terri Schiavo case).

Estate planning should only be done by attorneys, and it can be as simple as a Will, Health Care Documents, Living Will and Power of Attorney. It can also include a revocable, probate-avoidance trust, asset protection trusts, multi-generational tax-saving trusts, tax-saving charitable trusts, private family foundations, and many other fact-specific strategies.

Chapter 10: What is a Living Trust?

A trust is a contract between the Grantor (the person who creates the trust), the Trustee (one who controls the trust) and the beneficiaries (those entitled to benefit from the trust). You, as Grantor, determine how the trust will be operated by the Trustee and who benefits, how and when. You can create a trust that permits you to be Trustee and give yourself the right to receive full benefits from it. This type of trust is typically referred to as a Revocable Living Trust and is often used as a substitute to your Will. It permits you to keep total control and access to all your assets during your lifetime and provides for the distribution of your assets to your beneficiaries at your death. We often refer to a revocable living trust as your "Book of Instructions." A well-established advantage to Revocable Living Trusts is the avoidance of probate, which is required if you use a will to distribute your assets after death. Other advantages of Revocable Trusts, when property drafted, can include:

- Asset protection for your spouse after your death.
- Special needs planning for disabled beneficiaries.
- Asset management and protection for

children who are not proficient with handling money.

- Protection of assets from a spouse's subsequent remarriage after your death.
- Disability planning in the event you become disabled prior to death.
- Asset protection for your child if his or her marriage should fail to ensure your assets are not part of a divorce settlement.
- Keeping your affairs private (as opposed to open for public review in probate).
- No court intervention required (handled entirely by the Trustee you name in accordance with your detailed instructions).
- Plan for proper management of your business in your absence.

Very few revocable living trusts provide these benefits. Only a qualified estate planning attorney will know how to incorporate these protections into your plan. While a Revocable Living Trust has many advantages, it <u>does not</u> protect your assets from a nursing home, lawsuits, divorce bankruptcy or other creditor

Chapter 11: Do You Need to Avoid Probate?

What is probate?

It is the legal process of presenting your Will to the Court after your death to authenticate it and appoint your Executor. Your Executor must be appointed by the Court in order to collect and distribute your assets as stated in your Will. However, because it is a legal process, there are many steps that must be followed before your Executor can be appointed.

- The attorneys must obtain signatures from your heirs signifying they agree the Will is yours, and they will not contest it. Your heirs are your spouse and children, and <u>all</u> must agree not to contest your Will <u>before</u> your Executor can be appointed. If you don't have a spouse or child, probate becomes even more complicated. <u>Even</u> if your heir is not a beneficiary, his waiver is still required. This can be very different in second-marriage situations, if you have minor children or if you have a child, you have lost contact with. If a child dies before you, then all of your deceased child's children will have to agree not to contest your Will, but if they are under 18, the Court will need to appoint a separate attorney to represent them. The same is true if <u>any</u> of your heirs are legally incapacitated, such as a mentally disabled child or a spouse with Alzheimer's.

- The Executor will have to submit a family tree, filing fees, a petition, a death certificate and affidavits from the individuals who witnessed your Will. Upon receipt of all of the appropriate information (and if no heirs contest it), the Court will appoint the Executor.

- After your Executor is appointed, estate administration begins. It is a period of time the law permits the Executor to accumulate the assets and report to the Court how he or she intends to distribute them. This period is a minimum of * months after the Executor is appointed. However, in many cases, it can take a year or more. <u>If you die without a will</u>, the process is similar, but the State decides who gets your assets, not you.

- Unfortunately, probate is unpredictable. That's why many people chose to avoid it, but if all of your heirs agree and your assets are centralized, it can go smoothly.

Chapter 12: Why Estate Planning is not as Simple as it seems

This Could Happen to You?

Bob's parents and little brother are killed in an automobile crash. Mom had filled out a form so a "cheap" legal service would prepare wills for her and her husband. Somehow, they were never signed, and those unsigned wills named Mom's best friend as the guardian. Best friend convinced everyone she should be the one to take care of Bob. As soon as the life insurance policy and the automobile policy were part of Bob's estate, it was apparent that the best friend was only interested in the money. A painful guardianship battle ensued. It was clear that Dad had never liked Mom's best friend, and that the wills would have named a family member if only this family had met with an attorney. **Guardianships are essential.**

A couple just starting out with two children at home creates their own wills, using an Internet service. They leave everything to each other, and then to their children. Unfortunately, one dies of cancer, and the other dies in a work-related accident. The probate court is forced to require annual accountings and appearances. Much of their children's inheritance is paid to lawyers.

When each child turns 18, they receive what is left. $600,000.00 is too much for any 18 years old to handle. **A simple will is not enough.**

Grace's husband passes away; all the property is immediately hers because it was in joint tenancy. Her children quickly realize her memory is failing. She is not paying her bills or taking her medications. Dirk, her drug addict son, convinces her he is now clean and sober, and is the only child who loves her. He moves in, never lets her answer the phone, or allows his brothers or sisters to visit. He spends all moms' money on himself, uses her credit cards, and even gets new ones in his name. The other children finally go to Court, they paid the attorney's fees. Mom is left with no money and has suffered from malnutrition. **You need to protect your money while you are alive.**

Anne was widowed when her children were in High School. It took a long time, but she finally found a job. She was able to help her children go to college. She wanted to make sure that her children would have something when she was gone. She prudently purchased life insurance. Her son married a very wise and prudent woman, but her daughter married a man who loved expensive toys (plasma T.V., sports cars, and expensive wine). Anne was blessed with four grandchildren from her daughter. Anne was saving up money to help pay for her grand-children's education. She passed away before her oldest grandchild graduated from High School. Her estate passed easily to her two children through her living trust. Her daughter spent the inheritance she received on toys for her husband. When her daughter's children were ready for college there was no money left to pay for it. **You may want an inheritance protection trust to protect your children or grandchildren.**

Chapter 13: What if You … Die or become Disabled

What if…? I know you don't want to think about it, and yet I know you do. You worry and worry. When I sit with a family we talk about "what if". Planning for what if is the most important thing any family can do. I have lived through many what ifs. How many what ifs have you lived through?

 Have you planned for what ifs? What if you die? What if you are disabled and unable to take care of yourself? What if you have dementia? These are questions you don't want to ask. Procrastination is the most common estate planning mistake. We all want to put off thinking of bad things; we hope if we ignore them, they will go away. Of course, when death, disability, or dementia hit your home if you aren't ready the only option is Court. The Court proceedings related to death, disability and death are expensive and humiliating. Avoiding Court requires planning.

You may be surprised that 80% of all Trusts fail: they fail to avoid probate, fail to plan for disability or to avoid Conservatorship, and fail to avoid the loss of inheritances to creditors and predators and divorce. Why do Trusts fail? The law changes and as the law changes your Trust needs to be changed. Families change, most families realize the importance of protecting an inheritance from creditors, predators and divorce. Circumstances change, families sense a loved one's memory is failing or realize that a child will always need help. Very few Trusts contain any plan for dementia or disability. It is six times more likely that you will become disabled this year than that you will die. Will your family be able to take care of you if you are unable to care for yourself? Is your Trust out of date?

If you don't come home what will happen to your children? Who will be their guardian? Will they lose their inheritance to creditors, predators or divorce? What about your spouse? Will your spouse remarry? If your spouse remarries everything you worked for might go to the new wife or husband. What if you are disabled? Who will take care of you?

Chapter 14: Lessons learned from a Failed Trust

For several years, my husband, together with his brother and sister-in-law, had discussed their concern about my mother-in-law. She did not seem to be doing well. She was forgetting things, yet she denied that her memory was failing. My dear father-in-law did everything he could to protect her dignity and cover for the memory loss, so we did not know how bad things were until my father in-law fell and broke his hip. Like many people with Dementia or Alzheimer's Disease, the severity of the memory loss is not apparent until some part of the fragile structure that enables them to function falls apart. My father-in-law's injury was such an event. It became immediately apparent that my mother-in law could not be left alone, could not pay the bills and could not care for her very modest estate.

At the time, my in-laws knew I was extremely busy with my career and my children. They did not want to burden me further, and as they were out of town, had their Living Trust created by another attorney. Eventually, the family needed to review this trust. I became involved, but nobody could find the original, or even a copy. Finally, we found a business card, and I contacted their Estate Attorney. He provided me with copies, for a charge of $230.00. Part of my inspiration for creating my Trust Loving Care (TLC) maintenance program is based on the trauma we all suffered when we did not know who did the Trust and where it was, as well as our resentment about having to pay for the copies. All of my clients are offered the opportunity each year to invite their Trustees to meet with me, and when they join the TLC program, their family is never charged for a copy of the Trust, or the call to me when their loved one passes away-and they, like my husband and brother, need to know what to do.

I wish I could say that the stress associated with this event ended with finding the attorney and getting a copy of the Trust. It did not. The Trust itself failed. Why? The Trust was ten years old, and the successor Trustee was my father-in-law's best friend, who at 82 was just not able to do the job. My mother in-law could not change the Trust since it was obvious she lacked the capacity to make legal decisions. Yet she believed that she was fine and did not want to see a doctor about her condition. We spoke to her primary care physician, who was more than willing to verify that she lacked capacity, but HIPAA prevented him from talking to another doctor, and like ALMOST EVERY TRUST NOT DRAFTED BY AN ELDER LAW ATTORNEY, this trust required two doctors to sign that she did not have capacity. So, despite the fact that it was obvious, we could not do anything unless we could get her to a doctor, and you cannot legally make someone go to a doctor. We ended up having to obtain a Conservatorship of her person and moved her to a Secured Memory Facility. When my father-in law passed away, and the Power of Attorney my brother-in law used to pay bills was no longer valid, the Trust failed again. Why? The bank had misinformed us, and their CD was not in the Trust, so we now are required to account for her money in Conservatorship Probate Court. All of this could have been avoided. Having seen firsthand the catastrophic results of inadequate planning, I am fully committed to making sure that my clients, and their families, will not have to go through what my family and I did.

Chapter 15: What is a Trust? Do I need One?

A Trust is a legal document, a contract between the person who makes the Trust (the Grantor or Settlor), and the Trustee and Successor Trustees. The Trustee and the Grantor can be the same person. A Trust works like a wagon. If you put your toys in the wagon, and pull it away, the wagon and the toys go together. The toys that aren't in the wagon stay where they are. The person who has the ability to pull the wagon is the person who decides where the wagon goes and what happens to the toys in the wagon. A trust only controls assets that are put in the trust. If an asset is not transferred into the Trust, then the asset is not controlled by the Trust. One of the jobs of the Estate Planning or Elder Law Attorney is to help you make sure that all your assets are in your trust and that any assets that are not in your trust have been left out by design and that there is a plan for those assets too.

Here are some questions about Wills and Trusts that I am often asked:

Q.   What is the difference between a Will and a Trust?

A.   A Will takes effect after you pass away. Generally, if your estate is over $150,000 and if you have a Will your estate may have to go through Probate. There are many types of trusts. A Living Trust is the type of Trust that most people have. Most Living Trusts are only designed to avoid probate, our office provides you with more options. In our office you will be provided with options that will enable you to truly protect your family. Our trusts plan for life, and protect your spouse, children and grandchildren from creditors and predators. If you have a Trust and have transferred your assets to the Trust, then your estate will not have to go through Probate.

Q.   What is Probate?

A.   Probate is a court process. Generally, there are several steps to the probate process. The court appoints a person to be in charge of the decedent's estate. This person is called the personal representative or executor. The personal representative gathers the decedent's assets; pays the decedent's appropriate bills; he or she may sell certain of the decedent's assets; files tax returns; and distributes the decedent's assets to the appropriate persons or entities. All of this is done under the court's supervision. In Probate both the attorney and the executor each receive fees set by statute, these fees can be very expensive, and with the fee set at 4% of the first $100,000.00 and 3% of the next $100,000.00 and 2% of the next $800,000.00, and attorneys are allowed to ask for extraordinary fees.

Q. Why do people want to avoid Probate?

A. Probate has become a bad word in our society. It can be a time consuming and costly process. Proper estate planning can avoid Probate. If you do need to go through the Probate process, our office can help you through every step of the process.

Q. What happens if I die without a Will?

A. In California, if you die without a Will, the State of California and the Superior Court will decide who will be in charge of your estate and who will inherit your estate.

WHAT EVER YOU DO YOU NEED A PLAN

Chapter 16: Old trust, no trust, wrong trust? Could your trust fail?

Many people who come into my office already have trusts. On average the Trusts brought into my office are about ten years old. Laws change, families change, and you change. A Trust should be reviewed every three to five years to make sure that it incorporates the most recent laws. Some changes in the law have little effect on existing trusts, others like the major changes in the laws related to estate taxes or the rules related to obtaining assistance from Veteran's Benefits or Medicaid (in California we call the program Medi-Cal) can affect everyone, even those with small estates.

Changes in the laws will affect the recommendations competent attorneys make to their clients. A trust which is a perfect solution for a family can be the wrong solution when laws change. For instance, when I became a lawyer, Estate Taxes were charged to estates larger than $650,000.00. Lawyers planning Estates prior to the law changing made sure that the first person to die would use up their Estate Tax Exemption, which would allow the second to die to have

$650,000 as their tax exemption. This was the planning most families needed. The downside is that when the first spouse died part of the assets stayed in the Trust, and two tax returns were needed. A further downside is that if the surviving spouse needs care in a Nursing Home the part set aside must be used for care before the person can qualify for Medi-Cal. Sadly, I know many widows who lost a spouse, and have this kind of Trust; when their spouse died they had about $750,000 in assets, today they have around the same amount and not only do not need the cumbersome trusts to avoid estate taxes, they also end up unable to save the money and get help from Medi-Cal to pay for the high cost of medical care.

It is extremely important that when your family changes due to death or divorce that you revise your Trust. A major family change will change how you want your assets distributed. A divorce changes what you own, and for most people when they divorce, they no longer wish their (former) spouse to receive all their assets when they die. If a child dies before a parent, this could change who you want to receive your assets when you die. In the event of the death of a child, you should have your Trust reviewed since even if you are sure that your assets will go to the right person. If your memory or health is failing, your Trust needs to be updated. In this situation it is extremely important that you have a plan. The sickest person is not always the person who passes first. The Alzheimer's association has found that 80% of caregivers die first. Most people are just like my in-laws, they have sweetheart Trusts (if I die my sweetheart takes over); this is great when your sweetheart is well, but if they are suffering from dementia or a disabling disease, they will not be able to take over. Unless you have planned for an easy transition when the caregiver spouse dies there will be difficulty. Your loved one may like my mother in-law be so distraught and confused that they do not trust anyone and will not allow anyone to take over, or they just may want to hold on to the job desperately wanting to keep what little control over their life that remains. Either way it is easier to deal with these issues while the caregiver is alive.

If you have no Trust, you are guaranteed Probate (average cost $25,000). No Trust guarantees when your memory fails and you can't remember to pay your bills; you will be under Conservatorship, the court proceeding to allow someone to care for you and your money while you are alive (average cost over $100,000). No Trust, no Will and no Plan: your assets will go to whomever the law dictates; someone you love may be left out. A Trust may not be the best option for you, but you do need a plan and a way for someone to legally handle your affairs. Ironically, if you are in the unfortunate situation where you don't have anyone you trust then you should plan all your affairs so that the Court WILL supervise them if you lose the ability to handle your own money, or when you or your loved one dies. Court may be expensive, but it is less expensive than losing everything to someone who steals your money. Sadly, I have lost count of all the stories I have heard, and all the Court cases I have seen or been involved in where the untrustworthy relatives have stolen everything leaving the elderly victim with no money to use to go after the thief. Sadly, the police and District Attorneys are rarely able to prosecute these crimes.

In my next chapter I will discuss the different kinds of Trusts. If you or a loved one uses Medi-Cal to pay for medical or nursing home care, the state will require that you pay back every dime spent. The State can and will require the beneficiaries of a "Living Trust", and wills to pay it all back from the estate. If a loved one is in a skilled nursing home a special "Medi-Cal" Trust can protect all the assets from the State. Medi-Cal planning can save thousands of dollars. Veterans can use a trust similar to the "Medi-Cal" Trust to qualify for Aid and Attendance benefits. If a loved one is disabled, a "Special Needs Trust" is necessary to provide maximum care, while not causing the loved one to lose valuable benefits.

Chapter 17: Different Trusts, Different Purposes

I mentioned that there are different kinds of Trusts, and there are many different kinds of Trusts each with a specific purpose. There are trusts specifically designed to avoid Estate and Capital Gains taxes allowing those with millions of dollars to pass money while minimizing all the taxes which apply to larger estates. There are Trusts designed to give money to Charities, and there are Trusts designed to care for pets. Each of these trusts has its place; I routinely have helped families with this kind of planning. However, the focus of what I do is to help middle class families with planning to pay for care. The Trusts I use most often are my Medi-Cal Compliant Asset Protection Trust, my Veteran Benefits Compliant Asset Protection Trust, my Medi-Cal and Veteran's Benefits Compliant Asset Protection Trust, and my Special Needs Trust.

The most frequent question I am asked is "I have a Trust, why do I need a new one?" This is a really good question. The answer I usually give is the traditional Living Trust is a revocable Trust and all the assets are available to pay for care now and available to pay back the State of California for any benefits received. Living Trusts are open boxes everything is available; if you need help paying for care, your Living Trust does nothing to help you. You will need a trust designed especially for this purpose, an Asset Protection Trust that protects your assets and enables you to get the help you need.

Medi-Cal and the Veteran's Administration have rules; their rules are not the same, but there are similarities in the programs. The main similarity is that both programs require low assets. The other similarity is that planning for one can require planning for the other, so it requires special knowledge that people like me who spend a lot of time on these matters and become Certified as Elder Law Attorneys know. When you know the rules, you know how to plan. The special Trusts I create comply with the rules set out by Medi-Cal and/or the Veteran's Administration so that people can get the assistance they need and retain most of their assets. A Special Needs Trust is designed especially for a person who will receive an inheritance and who needs to maintain their eligibility for benefits available to people with disabilities, or for those who have a special need for protection.

Unfortunately, for most regular folks, all of this is confusing. The documents look the same, and there are even ads saying "You don't need a lawyer to do a Living Trust"; well I won't say the ads are a lie, but the truth is you need a lawyer to tell you what you need, and most people do not know enough about trusts to know if their do it yourself document is adequate to meet their needs. I don't need a mechanic to change my oil, but I do need a mechanic to look at my car and tell me if everything on my car is okay and that I don't need to repair anything.

Chapter 18: Do I Really Need to Do a Special Kind of Trust for My Disabled Child?

The Wall Street Journal ran an article on October 9, 2008, "An Estate Plan Built for Special Needs"; and many of my clients and friends called me to tell me that the Wall Street Journal was saying exactly what I had been telling them! I am passionate about planning specifically for disabled children.

It is very sad when a disabled child outlives their parents. Parents are unique; they love their child unconditionally and care for them regardless of the challenge. This is particularly true of mothers. Women typically bear the burden of care for both their parents and their children. A disabled child continues to need their mother (and father) long after most children are caring for their own parents.

An Estate Plan for a "Special Needs Child" must be designed to maximize the public benefits available to provide medical care, and a stipend for food and shelter, providing funds for everything else. The first Special Needs Trust I ever did was for a lovely lady who had a son with Down Syndrome; she had cancer, and he still lived at home. We were able to plan so he could continue to live at home, while receiving a check from SSI. His medical care, which was extensive, was covered by Medicare and Medi-Cal, and her best friend who was the Trustee could make sure that the videos he loved were rented for him, and he had the comic books he loved so much.

The rules for these Trusts are rather complicated. Most attorneys do not understand this area of Law and believe that all you need to do is put in the right words. The right words are indeed critical, as a Trust for Special Needs should have instructions, so the Trustee knows what things the person loves, so that the comic books and videos and other pleasures of life are provided.

Grandparents, aunts and uncles who want to help by providing for the disabled person must make sure that they have an Estate Plan that provides for the special person in their life. The consequence of not planning correctly can be devastating. If my dear client had not planned for her son correctly, her house would have been sold, and her money used to pay for her son's medical care, food, and shelter. For the son, this would have meant losing everything he loved, his home, his friends, his comic books and videos.

If you have a child with a disability, and he or she receives money from a Settlement, an Inheritance or gift, these funds can quickly disqualify the child (or adult) from public benefits. It is important to talk to an attorney who understands the benefit programs specially designed for children and adults with disabilities.

Chapter 19: What happens if you lose your mind?

No one really loses their mind, but as you age your odds of succumbing to Alzheimer's or a related dementia increase, as do your chances of a stroke. These conditions can leave you vulnerable to abuse, losing valuable assets and to death, due to your neglect of yourself.

Unfortunately, few people think about the possibility that they will become mentally incapacitated. We worry about losing our minds when we can't find out keys, or lose our wallet or purse, and losing things is a sign that your mind is going, but most often it is just inattention to detail. Mental incapacity can be obvious as it was in my mother in-law's situation where she literally forgot that her husband had gone to the hospital and spent the night going from her bedroom to the kitchen and back because when he wasn't found in one room he must be in the other. This is what short term memory loss looks like. Short term memory loss comes with constantly repeating stories and questions, forgetting to eat, forgetting to pay bills and an inability to care for you.

There is a more subtle and insidious form of mental incapacity, which is a loss of judgment. Those who suffer from this will believe the scam artists. They will be sure that if they give the nice person some money it will be used to pay taxes on the money they won in a lottery, or they will buy a product that does not exist (like a phony oil well). A person can lose their ability to make logical decisions and have their memory intact making it difficult for family and friends to get them help, because this form of mental incapacity is not as well documented or as easily tested as the dementias that come with short term memory loss.

Dealing with a loved one who is mentally incapacitated is certainly one of the most difficult experiences of a lifetime. Whenever possible, we work with our clients to avoid the confrontational and often family-dividing legal remedy known as conservatorship.

Avoiding conservatorship issues should be one of your greatest motivators to see us for a comprehensive estate plan; so that in the event that you ever become incapacitated, no loved one will be faced with an adversarial court proceeding to have you declared incompetent.

A court-appointed conservatorship is a protective arrangement established by the legal system on behalf of a mentally incapacitated individual. Most frequently, conservatorships are established on behalf of older adults who have lost mental capacity due to senile dementia, major strokes, severe mental illness, or other conditions.

The Conservator of the person oversees making personal and medical decisions on behalf of a mentally incapacitated individual. The Conservator of the property oversees making financial decisions on behalf of such an individual. It is important to note that one person can serve as both Conservator of the person and of the property

I often help families establish conservatorships when an individual has lost mental capacity, and no one can lawfully act for him/her. This is a painful process. A Conservatorship can often be avoided by Estate Planning that goes beyond planning for what happens when you die but considers the possibility of mental incapacity (that you might lose your mind before you die).

If you don't have an Advance Health Care Directive, or Financial Power of Attorney; the doctors, bankers, and insurance agents who know you will not be able to legally allow your family to help you with the decisions you need to make. If you lose your ability to think logically and give the power to handle your finances to someone who uses it to steal from you or place you in a facility where you cannot leave; someone who is trustworthy will need to go to Court and establish a Conservatorship to protect you.

I cannot over-emphasize the importance of creating a plan where you have people you trust in charge of your legal, financial and healthcare decisions if you become mentally incapacitated. Bad people have a radar that enables them to find people having problems with their ability to think straight, if the people you trust have not been given permission to help you before this occurs, you may become a victim, and getting money back from bad guys is never easy. This is why Elder Law Attorneys like me spend so much time planning for "What happens if you don't die?".

Chapter 20: What is a Power of Attorney for Finances, why do I need it?

A durable power of attorney for property management is a written instrument by which one person called the "principal" authorizes another person called the "attorney in fact" to act as the principal's agent, notwithstanding the principal's subsequent incapacity. The document can give the attorney in fact the authority to make decisions concerning the principals' real property, investments, cash, bank accounts, and trust. The durable power of attorney can be very broad, giving the attorney in fact power over all the principal's assets, or narrow, giving the attorney in fact authority in fact power over specific assets.

If you become incapacitated, someone will need to manage your assets. If you become incapacitated, the court will be required to appoint a conservator to manage your assets, unless a written document like a trust or durable power of attorney for property management authorizes someone to make decisions for you regarding each of your assets. If you have a living trust, the successor trustee can manage all the assets held by the trust, but he or she cannot manage any asset that was not transferred into the trust. This is yet another reason a trust must be kept current.

There are two kinds of power of attorney: general and special. A general durable power of attorney enables the attorney in fact to act on behalf of the principal with respect to all matters. A person who believes he or she will shortly be unable to handle his or her own affairs because of a medical condition such as Alzheimer's disease, should execute a durable power of attorney for property management as promptly as possible, so that their competency to do so is not questioned. If the power of attorney gives the attorney in fact only limited authority, it is "special", and the attorney in fact has only the authority granted in the document.

A Power of Attorney can become effective at a date later than the date it is signed. A springing power of attorney is a durable power of attorney that only becomes effective when a certain specified event occurs. The majority of this type of Durable Power of attorney becomes effective only after the principal becomes incapacitated, although another event or contingency can be specified. There are several difficulties with this type of power of attorney. First, they are not authorized in some states. Second, they are viewed with more mistrust than a traditional durable power of attorney. Third, there is difficulty in determining whether the "triggering" event has occurred, even though California law authorizes the principle to designate a person whose written declaration under penalty of perjury determines conclusively that the specified event has occurred.

A spouse is often the best candidate, to be the Attorney in Fact. However, if a spouse is unsophisticated in handling business matters, or is too ill to handle the task, a third party maybe a better choice. If your spouse is unable, or unwilling, (or you are not married), you may choose anyone to serve as your attorney in fact. In choosing this person, you MUST keep in mind that this person must be trustworthy. **A DURABLE POWER OF ATTORNEY FOR PROPERTY MANAGEMENT IS THE EQUIVALENT OF A BLANK CHECK.** If the person you choose as your agent is not a family member, you should consider a provision in the document that provides for them to be compensated.

A California Uniform Statutory Form Power of Attorney is available at most stationery and office supply forms. If the form is completed by you alone or at the suggestion of a friend of family member you may give too much Power to the wrong person or cause adverse tax consequences. A Power of Attorney is NOT just a form, it is a document that entrusts someone with all your money. It is a blessing in the right hands, and a curse in the wrong hands. It can be used to take all your money. An attorney should always be consulted before signing a Power of Attorney, and the Attorney should make sure that you understand the document and that you are the person who will benefit from giving this power away.

Chapter 17: Health Care- What Do You Want at End of Life?

Health Care Decisions how can someone help.

I frequently hear concerns from clients, colleagues and friends that they don't want to live for months hooked up to machines, yet they also want the best medical care if there is hope of recovery, and a few more years on earth. As illness or age increase the greatest concern is that CPR will be used, and that life will be prolonged.

I am providing these materials to assist you in meeting the legal requirements to make your wishes known; and to provide you with the documents you need to ensure that medical personnel will follow your wishes.

The first document you need to know about is an ADVANCE HEALTH CARE DIRECTIVE.

What is an Advance Health Care Directive?

An "Advance Health Care Directive" is the form which under California law allows you to appoint another person to be your health care "agent". This person will have the legal authority to make decisions about your medical care if you become unable to make these decisions for yourself. An "Advance Health Care Directive" allows you to write down your health care wishes, and your doctor and your agent must follow your lawful instructions.

An "Advance Health Care Directive" is highly recommended. In today's medical environment, doctors are very reluctant to listen to any family member who does not have written authority to act on your behalf. Family members who have a written document with your desires on it have both the legal authority to act, and confidence in acting because your wishes are written for them.

Do I need a "living will"?

The term "living will" was the general term which encompassed the Natural Death Act Declaration and other documents which allowed a person to state that they did not desire life sustaining treatment if they are terminally ill or permanently unconscious. An "Advance Heath Care Directive" is now the legally recognized format for a "living will"; it replaces the Natural Death Act Declaration AND allows you to state your desires about your health care in any situation which you are unable to make your own decisions.

You will not need any additional documents; the "Advance Health Care Directive" contains a statement regarding your wishes about life-sustaining treatment.

What if I already have a "Durable Power of Attorney or Natural Death Act Declaration?

If you have a Durable Power of Attorney for Health Care executed before 1992; it has expired and should be replaced. All other valid Durable Powers of Attorney and Natural Death Act Declarations remain valid.

The new "Advance Health Care Directive" gives you more flexibility, and by combining the designation of your agent with the statements regarding life-sustaining treatment it makes it simpler for your agent to act. At a minimum you should review your existent Durable Power of Attorney for Health Care or Natural Death Act Declaration to make sure it has not expired and that it still accurately reflects your wishes.

What are the legal requirements for completing an Advance health Care directive?

Any California resident who is at least eighteen (18) years old (or is an emancipated minor), of sound mind, and acting of his or her own free will can complete a valid Advance Health care Directive.

The document may be acknowledged before a notary public in California or two adult witnesses who are not appointed as your health care agents. These witnesses cannot be a health care provider or an employee of a health care provider, or an operator or an employee of a care facility for the elderly.

If a person is in a skilled nursing facility the document must be witnessed by an Ombudsman, and the telephone number of the Ombudsman must be posted at the facility.

Who should I appoint?

You can appoint any adult except your doctor, or a person who operates a facility (board and care home, residential care facility, or nursing home). However, they can be appointed if that person is related to you by blood, marriage or adoption, or is your co-worker.

The person you select should be someone you trust, and someone who has the ability to speak up for you. You should select someone who understands your wishes, and who is willing to accept this responsibility.

You may select one or more agents, who should be listed to act one at a time.

How much authority will my health care agent have?

Your agent has legal authority to speak for you in all health care matters. Health care professionals will look to your agent for decisions rather than your next of kin or any other persons. Your agent will be able to accept or refuse medical treatment, have access to your medical records, and make decisions about donating your organs, authorizing an autopsy, and disposing of your body should you die. The agent may not legally authorize convulsive treatment, psychosurgery, sterilization, abortion or placement in a mental health treatment facility.

If you do not want your agent to have all these powers, you can write a statement in the Advance Health Care Directive form limiting your agent's authority. Your agent must make decisions consistent with any instructions you have written in the Advance Health Care Directive form.

What if I change my mind after completing and Advance Health Care Directive?

You can revoke or change an Advance Health Care Directive at any time. To revoke the entire form, including the appointment of your agent, you must inform all health care providers who have a copy of the of Advance Health care Directive in writing, and complete a new Advance Health Care Directive which should state that the previous directive was revoked.

How will emergency personnel (such as paramedics) find my Advance Health Care Directive form in the event of an emergency?

You need to be sure that the Advance health Care Directive is kept in an obvious place, and that your agent has a copy. If you specifically do not want to be Resuscitated, a Do not Resuscitate form is also included with this information. To be effective the form must be signed by your physician. You should order a medic alert bracelet so that paramedics know immediately your wishes. Paramedics rarely look at wallets.

Is an Advance Health Care Directive valid in other States?

If you spend a lot of time in another state you should consult lawyer in that State, if you are traveling, most states will recognize an Advance Health Care directive that is executed legally in another State, but they are not required by law to honor it.

A GUIDE TO DETAILING YOUR WISHES

In order to assist you in making these decisions, I have developed some question which will help you to describe how you feel.

Describe what medical care if any you want to receive if you were in a coma, and your life expectancy was not certain?

How do you feel about being fed by a tube, when you no longer can eat?

If you are permanently unable to recognize and communicate with people, and you an able to feel pain, and are aware of your surroundings, how much medical care would you want? If you contracted an illness (such as pneumonia, urinary tract infection, etc.) that could be cured or reversed would you want care to cure the illness?

If you have a disease or condition that cannot be cured, and you are told that you will die within six months, what kind of medical care do you want? If you contracted an illness (such as pneumonia, urinary tract infection, etc.) that could be cured or reversed would you want care to cure the illness?

Are there any medical conditions your family should know about?

Do you have any special requests regarding burial, or your funeral service?

WHAT WOULD YOU WANT YOUR FAMILY TO DO IF YOU WERE LIKE TERRI SCHIAVO?

Most of you have heard about and seen Terri Schiavo. For those of us who don't remember, Teri suffered a heart attack, and after heroic measures to save her, she was in a coma described as a persistent vegetative state. She woke up and appeared to be able to see and hear. Everyone had an opinion, and it was heart wrenching to watch as her husband and parents fought over her fate. No one really knows what Terri Schiavo really wanted, because she never wrote it down. A conservative republican Judge found the evidence presented by her husband that she would not want to be artificially kept alive clear and convincing, and the power to make the decision was given to her husband. Terri Schiavo was being kept alive through the artificial administration of food and hydration. She was a shy woman who never would have wanted to have her life and death the center of world attention. No one I know would want such a private matter made into such a public spectacle. After the Court allowed her husband to remove the artificial food and hydration, and an autopsy was performed the coroner found that her brain was like Jell-O and that she could not see and that the waking was a reflex, and that she only appeared to know that someone was nearby.

As an elder law attorney, I understand how important it is to put in writing what you would want done if you were terminally ill, in a coma, or persistent vegetative state. I advise clients on their options, and draft specific instructions for their family. You are never too young to think about what you would want your family to do if a tragedy occurred and decisions needed to be made. If your family must decide for you, they need to know what you want, I can prepare you to have that talk with your family. If you have an advance healthcare document prepared your family can have peace of mind that they honored your wishes, they will have in writing your philosophy of death and dying. Most people have strong opinions on this subject; many have deeply held religious convictions. I don't "just" provide my clients with Advance Healthcare Directives ("Living Wills"), I also provide them with the advice and information they need to provide direction to their family when the time comes, and their family must decide what to do when their loved one is in the hospital and not able to communicate their desires

Chapter 21: Paying for Nursing Home Care

MEDI-CAL PLANNING

Many courts have commented that federal Medicaid laws are the most complicated law that have ever been promulgated by Congress. In California, the Medicaid program is called Medi-Cal, and there are many special laws, rules, regulations and interpretations which increase the confusion.

There are two major categories of Medi-Cal benefits, one pays for medical care for the truly indigent, and the other pays for Skilled Nursing Care in a facility licensed to provide for this level of care, i.e. a nursing home. Providing for care and preserving assets require careful planning, and a clear focus that we must always make sure we have the best interests of the person facing the need for care as our primary focus.

For most of us, our biggest asset is our home. Most people want their home to go to their children when we pass, we certainly don't want our home or our assets to go to the State of California. With proper planning, a home can be protected, and you need not lose your home to pay for care.

The State of California does everything it can to recover the money from the estates of the people it has spent on their nursing home care; it is ruthless and relentless in this recovery pursuit. When your family plans to preserve assets while having the State of California through Medi-Cal pay for your loved one's skilled nursing care; you must have as part of your planning strategy prevention of the State of California getting repayment from you, their heirs. The rules for avoiding recovery are far more complex than the rules for qualifying for Medi-Cal. It is important to seek the advice of a person who is keeping up to date on the myriads of rules and regulations being promulgated by the State.

If you as a loved one are facing the need for care, you should seek advice from a qualified Elder Law Attorney as soon as you find out that care in the home is no longer an option. The sooner you seek advice the better; early planning gives you the most possible choices available. I am available to assist you with Medi-Cal Planning

Veteran's Benefits to Pay for Care

What Are Aid and Attendance Benefits?
Aid and Attendance is a benefit paid by Veterans Affairs (VA) to veterans, veteran spouses or surviving spouses. It is paid in *addition* to a veteran's basic pension. The benefit may not be paid without eligibility to a VA basic pension. Aid and Attendance is for applicants who need financial help for in–home care, or to pay for an assisted living facility or a nursing home. It is a non–service-connected disability benefit, meaning the disability does not have to be a result of service. You cannot receive non–service and service–connected compensation at the same time.

Aid and Attendance benefits are paid to those applicants who:

- Are eligible for a VA pension
- Meet service requirements
- Meet certain disability requirements
- Meet income and asset limitations

Basic Eligibility for VA Benefits

1. Be a veteran who served at least 90 days of active duty or the surviving spouse of a wartime veteran (married at the time of veteran's death)
2. At least one day of active duty had to be during wartime:
   WWII –   12/07/1941 to 07/25/1947
   Korea –   06/27/1950 to 12/31/1955
   Vietnam – 08/05/1964 to 05/07/1975
   (02/28/1961-05/07/1975 if in
   Vietnam proper)
3. Does not need to have been in combat
4. Discharged other than dishonorably

   - Honorable discharge
   - Discharge under honorable conditions
   - General Discharge
   - Bad conduct discharge, Discharge under other than honorable conditions, or Undesirable discharge may still be eligible after a "character of service determination" hearing

Chapter 22: Nine Common and Costly Estate Planning Mistakes

Mistakes are part of life. Some mistakes can be life threatening. Fortunately, some mistakes can be avoided or eliminated by thinking ahead; So, it is with estate planning mistakes. This is a warning about the most common mistakes; the list is **not** exclusive.

1. Procrastination: Most people have no plan at all. Who wants to face the possibility of their future incapacity and the certainty of their death? It is an ugly proposition. Nevertheless, only you can make your estate plan a top priority. Otherwise, you expose yourself, your loved ones and your hard-earned assets to probate and avoidable death taxes. Take time to carefully think through, implement and then update your estate plan. You and your loved ones will be glad you did.

2. Not planning for Incapacity: Too many people think estate planning relates to distributing assets after death. Total estate planning begins with planning for your own incapacity (the day when your mind fails). Adults are required to make their own personal, health care and financial decisions. If you have not given someone permission to make these decisions for you, a probate judge will be required to appoint someone who will make the decisions for you. The process of having a court name someone for you is painful and extremely expensive.

3. No back-up Parents: Most parents consider their children to be their most valuable assets. These parents often devote considerable time and treasure to providing educations, activities and religious training for their children. Incredibly, these same parents typically fail to legally appoint guardians for their minor children in the event both parents die. When back up parents are not selected in writing prior to death great hardship and even custody battles can ensue between well-meaning friends or relatives.

4. Winding up in Probate Court: Many people overlook simple steps to ensure that their estate -or at least a big chunk of it –avoids being processed through probate court. Probate proceedings can drag on for months or even years and can eat up to 5 percent or more of an estate's value. Contact and consult with an Estate Planning Attorney in order to avoid probate, and avoid risks created by techniques such as joint tenancy which expose you to the possibility that the person you add to title on your property or bank account will take your assets.

5. No Inheritance Protection: No one values a dollar like the person who earned it. If you do not incorporate *inheritance protection* into your estate planning, your hard-earned assets could be squandered by your surviving spouse's new spouse, your or their children or grandchildren, or lost to heir divorces, lawsuits or bankruptcies. Enough said.

6. Keeping Poor Records: One of the biggest mistakes people make is not regularly updating their estate plans. Every two or three years, blow the dust off your estate plan and go through it. When estate plans are old, children are more likely to argue about what dad or mom really intended, which can cause horrible fights and destruction of family relationships. Sometimes an out-of-date estate plan names people who are no longer alive, or worse, fail to name new members of the family.

7. No Estate Tax Planning: Many people think the Estate Tax cannot possibly apply to them. It is common for people to be surprised at how much they actually own after they make a list of all their assets including life insurance. You may not think your estate is big enough or that estate taxes will go away but if you guess wrong, and you do not plan to avoid estate taxes, the IRS could assess your heirs hundreds of thousands of dollars, much of which could have been avoided.

8. Being Disorganized: It is not uncommon for a family struck with grief, or finally admitting mom or dad cannot handle their personal business; to find they have no idea of what a loved one owns, where their Will or Trust is, or where the safety deposit box or key is. When files are in a shambles, relatives can spend weeks or months tracking down assets. Leaving a disorganized estate can also dramatically inflate legal bills after a death, regardless of the size of the estate.

9. Failing to make Special Plans for Disabled Children: Once a disabled child becomes an adult, they will receive essential government benefits. If they receive an inheritance, they can be disqualified from receiving these benefits. A "special Needs Trust" can be set up as part of your estate plan to make sure that they can receive their benefits while a trustee can ensure that they receive the things that make them comfortable and happy. If you leave a disabled child's inheritance to their brother's and sister's, the disabled child's inheritance is not protected. Planning ahead will give your disabled child a good life even when you are gone.

"An Ounce of Prevention
is worth a Pound of Cure"

"Now What"

You have been presented with admittedly a daunting amount of information and numbers. Perhaps you are feeling overwhelmed, I know my husband and brother-in-law did as they dealt with the tragic discovery of their mother starting on the road of Alzheimer's. Perhaps you now have many more questions than answers. That is where I come into the picture. I am here to help you through this process. I am sure you have found this book useful, but I also know that there is nothing like talking face to face. Since I know you want to plan for your family, so you are prepared for all the "What if's" of life and death, please don't hesitate to give me a call at (855) ELDER77 or (855)353-3777. I enjoy helping people and guiding them as they make the decisions necessary to make sure that families are prepared for life, dementia, disability, disease, as well as death. I guarantee that I will provide you with the most current legal solutions for your situation.

This book was written by

Martha Jo Geisler Patterson, J.D., CELA
certified by the National Elder Law Foundation

Published by Geisler Patterson Law

Mailing Address
1400 N. Kraemer Blvd. #1494, Placentia, CA
92871

Phone: 855 ELDER-77 or 855.353.3777

Email: mjplawmom@gmail.com

And on the web at: www.ElderLawMom.com

www.ingramcontent.com/pod-product-compliance
Lightning Source LLC
Chambersburg PA
CBHW070443240526
45479CB00014B/671